FOXES

by Mary Ann McDonald

Published in the United States of America by The Child's World®
1980 Lookout Drive • Mankato, MN 56003-1705
800-599-READ • www.childsworld.com

PHOTO CREDITS
© blickwinkel/Alamy: 13
© Colin Seddon/naturepl.com: 15
© David W. Hamilton/Getty Images: 8
© Helen Williams/Photo Researchers, Inc.: 6–7
© Image Source Pink/Alamy: 16–17
© iStockphoto.com/Graeme Purdy: cover, 1
© iStockphoto.com/stanfair: 3, 31
© Jose Schell/naturepl.com: 5
© Kevin Schafer/Corbis: 18
© Loetscher Chlaus/Alamy: 27
© Patrick J. Endres/Visuals Unlimited: 28
© tbkmedia.de/Alamy: 22–23
© Terry Whittaker/Alamy: 11
© Thomas & Pat Leeson/Photo Researchers, Inc.: 21
© Tim Wright/Corbis: 24–25
© Yva Momatiuk/John Eastcott/Minden Pictures: 9

ACKNOWLEDGMENTS
The Child's World®: Mary Berendes, Publishing Director;
Katherine Stevenson, Editor; Pamela Mitsakos, Photo Researcher;
Judy Karren, Fact Checker

The Design Lab: Kathleen Petelinsek, Design and Page Production

LIBRARY OF CONGRESS CATALOGING-IN-PUBLICATION DATA
McDonald, Mary Ann.
  Foxes / by Mary Ann McDonald.
    p. cm. — (New naturebooks)
  Includes index.
  ISBN-13: 978-1-59296-845-9 (library bound : alk. paper)
  ISBN-10: 1-59296-845-7 (library bound : alk. paper)
  1. Foxes—Juvenile literature. I. Title.
  QL737.C22M383 2007
  599.775—dc22   2006103443

Table of Contents

On the cover: This red fox is hunting at sunset in Great Britain.

Meet the Fox!

Red foxes can run as fast as 30 miles (48 km) an hour.

A fox can curl its bushy tail around itself at night to stay warm. The tail also helps the fox stay balanced as it runs and turns.

On a cold winter's night, you sit at the edge of a meadow. You bring your hand up to your mouth and breathe through your fingers. You make a noise that sounds like an injured rabbit. You make the noise again, and then you sit and watch. Out of nowhere, an animal appears at the far end of the meadow. It is furry, with a long, bushy tail. The animal looks around, and then it disappears again. What could this creature be? It's a fox!

This red fox is watching for food near its home on Canada's Anticosti Island.

What Do Foxes Look Like?

Foxes, like cats, have sensitive whiskers on their faces. The whiskers help them find out about their surroundings. They can even feel tiny movements of animals in the grass.

Foxes lick and groom their fur to keep it clean.

Foxes have triangle-shaped ears, pointed noses, and bushy tails. In fact, they look a lot like small dogs. That's because foxes and dogs belong to the same animal group. They are both canids (KAY-nidz). Wolves and coyotes are canids, too. All canids are warm-bodied **mammals** that have fur-covered bodies and feed their babies milk.

Foxes are known for their beautiful, thick coats. The color of a fox's fur is very important—it helps the fox hide! Many foxes are colored to look like the dirt and rocks around them. This protective coloring is called **camouflage**. It makes the fox very hard to see.

The color of this swift fox's fur helps it blend in with the leaves and rocks near its home.

6

This arctic fox has its summer coloring. You can see how it blends in with the nearby rocks.

Many foxes grow heavier coats to keep them warm in the winter. In the spring, they shed the extra fur and are left with a lighter summer coat. Sometimes their coloring changes a bit with the seasons. But the arctic fox changes color completely! This fox lives in snowy areas of the far north. In winter, when the snow is on the ground, the fox is white to blend in. During the late winter and spring, it loses its winter coat and turns gray or brown to match the ground. It turns white again in the fall.

Arctic foxes have small ears, short legs, and the warmest fur of any mammal. They are able to stay warm even when the temperature is far below zero.

Some other arctic animals turn white for the winter, too, including ptarmigans and snowshoe hares.

This arctic fox has its winter coat. You can see how well it blends in with the snow.

Are There Different Kinds of Foxes?

Foxes that live in deserts have short fur and big ears. The ears not only hear well, they also help the foxes' bodies get rid of extra heat.

Australia didn't used to have any foxes. In the 1800s, people took red foxes there so they could hunt them. Now the foxes are pests that harm farm animals and wildlife.

There are over 20 different kinds, or **species**, of foxes. They come in many different sizes and colors. They're found in almost every part of the world except Antarctica. Red foxes, with their reddish fur and darker legs, are the most common and best known. They live throughout most of North America and in other parts of the world, too. Gray foxes have shorter legs and gray fur. They're well known throughout the U.S. and Mexico. Arctic foxes live only in the far north. Swift foxes and kit foxes are smaller types from grasslands and deserts of western North America. Fennec foxes of Africa's Sahara Desert are one of the smallest kinds. They weigh only 2 to 3 pounds (about 1 kg).

You can see how this gray fox differs from the red fox on page 5.

What Are Foxes' Dens Like?

Some arctic-fox dens are huge, with dozens of entrances. The dens can be up to 300 years old. Arctic foxes sometimes dig tunnels in the snow, too.

Gray foxes have sharp, hooked claws and can climb trees. Their dens are sometimes in hollow trees.

No matter where on Earth they live, all foxes make use of dens. The dens are safe places where the foxes can rest, raise their babies, or escape from enemies. They keep the foxes warm and dry when the weather is bad—or shaded and cool if it is hot. A fox might have over a dozen dens throughout its **territory**. Foxes make their dens in hollow logs, under big rocks, and under fallen trees. Sometimes they even dig tunnels into the ground.

Here you can see a red fox as it peeks out of its den in Switzerland.

What Do Foxes Eat?

Foxes that live near people sometimes go through trash cans or gardens looking for food.

Arctic foxes sometimes follow polar bears and eat leftover scraps from their kills.

Foxes are **predators** that hunt other animals for food. The animals they eat are called their **prey**. Foxes eat many kinds of prey, especially small animals such as mice, shrews, ground squirrels, and voles. Foxes also eat insects, earthworms, small rabbits, birds, eggs, and lizards. Sometimes they even eat berries and other fruits.

Foxes are also **scavengers**. That means they'll eat almost anything they can find—even dead animals. By eating dead animals, called **carrion**, foxes help keep the countryside clean.

This red fox has caught a pheasant to eat.

14

How Do Foxes Hunt?

Foxes can smell food from a mile (over a kilometer and a half) away—sometimes even if it is buried under snow.

Foxes see very well at night.

Foxes are very good hunters. Unlike some canids, they don't hunt in packs. Usually they hunt alone. They have keen hearing and an excellent sense of smell. A fox often sneaks up on its prey by crawling on its belly. It must be very quiet and patient. When it gets close enough, the fox pounces quickly. It pins its prey to the ground with its paws. Then it's time to eat!

Foxes are mostly **nocturnal** animals. That means they are active at night and rest during the day. At night, the foxes' prey are active, too. If foxes hunted during the day, they probably wouldn't find as much food.

This red fox is chasing a mink through the snow.

16

Sometimes a fox catches more food than it can eat. When this happens, it takes the extra food to a safe place and buries it. Some foxes bury their food right in the ground. Others cover it with sticks or leaves. By burying their food, the foxes try to keep other animals from stealing it. When the fox is hungry again, it digs up its meal and starts eating!

Storing extra food is especially important in winter, when food can be hard to find.

Arctic foxes store up food during the summer. The food freezes and helps keep the animals fed through the long, cold winter.

Here you can see a red fox as it buries some leftover food in Utah's Uinta National Forest.

19

What Are Baby Foxes Like?

Foxes often mate for life.

Arctic foxes have the largest litters of any wild mammal. They often have 11 kits. Litters of 22 have been recorded.

A male fox is called a *dog fox*. A female is called a vixen. During the late winter, the dog fox and vixen mate. Then they look for a den that is safe, quiet, and big enough for a family. They make sure the den is warm, clean, and dry. When spring comes, the vixen fives birth to her **litter** of babies, called *kits*. The number of kits depends on the type of fox.

These young fox kits live in a hollow tree.

When the kits are born, they're helpless and weak and cannot see. Both parents take care of them. The kits grow quickly, and after about a month, they peek outside for the first time. For several weeks their only food is their mother's milk. Then they start eating food their parents bring back. Slowly the kits grow stronger. When they are about four months old, the kits learn how to hunt. By the end of the summer, they have grown big and strong. They are ready to go live on their own.

These older fox kits are playing outside their den. They live in a forest in Germany.

Kits spend a lot of their time playing tag and pouncing on each other. That helps them learn to run, chase, and hunt.

Sometimes young foxes stay with their parents for a while, helping them raise the next batch of kits.

23

How Do Foxes Communicate?

Fox parents makes a coughing sound to tell their kits danger is near.

Foxes communicate over long distances with some sounds. They use other sounds to communicate when they are together.

Foxes communicate with each other in many different ways. They leave smells on trees, grasses, and rocks. The smells help them mark their territories. Foxes also move their bodies and tails to show when they are happy, angry, or frightened. But the most important way foxes talk to each other is by using sounds.

Foxes can make many different sounds. Each sound means a different thing. Some sounds mean "Here I am!" Others say "Danger!" By barking, whining, yipping, and growling, foxes tell each other what is going on and how they feel.

These gray foxes are communicating by sniffing each other and touching noses.

24

Are Foxes in Danger?

Like many other animals, foxes sometimes get a deadly disease called *rabies*.

People's dogs that run loose can kill foxes, give them diseases, or compete with them food.

Coyotes, eagles, and bobcats are all enemies of foxes. But a fox's most dangerous enemy is people. For thousands of years, people have hunted and trapped foxes for their beautiful fur. People have also hunted them for sport. Foxes eat lots of really troublesome pests, such as mice. But some farmers think of them as chicken-eating pests and kill them. Sometimes people leave out poisons for other animals, and foxes eat the poison by mistake. Many foxes are also hit by cars.

People harm foxes in other ways, too. More people keep moving into areas where foxes live. Building roads and houses destroys the foxes' living areas.

This red fox lives on Alaska's Augustine Island.

Some kinds of foxes, such as red foxes and gray foxes, are still doing well. But a few kinds are in real trouble. The Darwin's fox, which lives only near the coast of Chile, is listed as **endangered**. So is California's island fox. Some kinds of swift foxes are in trouble, too. Sometimes local populations of foxes are in danger even if the species is doing well overall.

We still have lots to learn about these clever, quick hunters. If you keep your eyes open, you might see foxes living near you!

Foxes could live as long as 15 years, but in the wild, they usually only live three or four.

Some kinds of foxes get used to living near people. In fact, sometimes they live near or even in big cities.

This red fox is keeping a close eye on the photographer!

Glossary

camouflage (KA-muh-flazh) Camouflage is special coloring or markings that help an animal blend in with its surroundings. Foxes' fur can act as camouflage.

carrion (KAYR-ee-un) Carrion is the rotting meat of dead animals. Foxes eat carrion.

endangered (in-DAYN-jurd) An endangered animal is one that is close to dying out completely. Some kinds of foxes are endangered.

litter (LIH-tur) A litter is a group of babies born to one animal at the same time. Foxes have several babies in a litter.

mammals (MAM-ullz) Mammals are warm-blooded animals that have hair on their bodies and feed their babies milk from the mother's body. Foxes are mammals.

nocturnal (nok-TUR-nul) An animal that is nocturnal is active mostly at night and rests during the day. Foxes are nocturnal.

predators (PREH-duh-turz) Predators are animals that hunt and kill other animals for food. Foxes are predators.

prey (PRAY) Prey are animals that other animals hunt as food. Mice are common prey for foxes.

scavengers (SKA-vun-jurz) Animals that are scavengers will feed on whatever garbage they find, including dead animals. Foxes are scavengers.

species (SPEE-sheez) An animal species is a group of animals that share the same features and can have babies only with animals in the same group. There are over 20 species of fox.

territory (TEHR-uh-tor-ee) An animal's territory is the area that the animal claims as its own and defends against outsiders. Foxes mark their territories with smells.

To Find Out More

Read It!

Macdonald, David W. *Foxes*. Stillwater, MN: Voyageur Press, 2000.

Mason, Cherie, and Jo Ellen McAllister Stammen (illustrator). *Wild Fox: A True Story*. Camden, ME: Down East Books, 1993.

Perry, Phyllis J. *Crafty Canines: Coyotes, Foxes, and Wolves*. New York: Franklin Watts, 1999.

Tweit, Susan J., and Wendy Shattil (photographer). *City Foxes*. Denver, CO: Denver Museum of Natural History; Portland, OR: Alaska Northwest Books, 1997.

Woods, Shirley E., and Celia Godkin (illustrator). *Amber: The Story of a Red Fox*. Markham, Ont.: Fitzhenry & Whiteside, 2004.

On the Web

Visit our Web page for lots of links about foxes:
http://www.childsworld.com/links

Note to Parents, Teachers, and Librarians: We routinely check our Web links to make sure they're safe, active sites—so encourage your readers to check them out!

31

Index

About the Author

Mary Ann McDonald is a professional wildlife photographer who lives in central Pennsylvania with her husband Joe, also a photographer and writer. For the past 17 years, she has photographed wildlife around the world from Rwanda to Chile to Yellowstone National Park. Mary Ann and Joe teach photography workshops at their home, which they call Hoot Hollow. Mary Ann's photographs have appeared in many national and international publications, including Ranger Rick, Your Big Back Yard *and* National Geographic Kids.